María and the Baker's Bread

A Peruvian Folk Tale

Retold by Daphne Liu

Illustrated by Martha Aviles

HAMPTON-BROWN

Characters

María

The baker

María and the baker have a problem. What do you think it is?

María and the Baker's Bread

María Serafina Graciela Mamani lives in a small town in Peru. She has a long name and many friends.

María feeds the farmer's chickens. He gives María some of his eggs.

María stirs the cook's pots. The cook gives María some of her tasty stew.

María picks the neighbor's fruit. The neighbor gives María some of his sweet mangoes.

Everyone's Friend

Song

She gathers the farmer's eggs.

She stirs the cook's hot stew.

She picks the neighbor's mangoes.

She always knows what to do.

She carries the lady's basket.

She catches the old man's hat.

She brushes the little girl's hair.

She does good things like that!

Every day, María walks by the bakery.
She wants to buy bread, but she does not
have any money. So she takes a deep breath
and enjoys the smell.

Every day, the baker frowns. He says,
"María Mamani, you should pay me for
the smell of my bread!"

One day, the baker gets very angry.
"María Mamani," he shouts, "you smell
my bread every day. You must pay me.
Give me three gold coins!"

María smiles. "You can make me pay for what I eat. But you cannot make me pay for what I smell!"

Everyone agrees.

Baker's Song

I wake up early every morning.
I bake my bread so sweet.
My wife bakes lots of cakes
   and rolls.
 We sell our tasty treats.

You stand outside our window.
You smell our bread each day.
You use your nose to steal
   from us.
It is YOUR turn to pay!

María does not pay the baker. Every day she goes back to the bakery and smells the baker's bread.

And now, María's friends go, too! They all smell the bread together.

Finally, the baker yells, "María Mamani! I will take you to the judge. He will make you pay for the smell of my bread!"

María is afraid! She does not have money to pay the baker.

María's friends say, "Don't worry!"

Well, maybe she should worry a *little* bit!

The next day, María goes to the courtroom.
Its seats are filled with her friends.

The baker tells his story. "I work hard! She smells my bread for free!"

María tells her story. "I love the smell of his bread. But I cannot pay."

The judge says, "Your problem is interesting. I will think about it and give my answer soon."

The judge is a very good thinker.

Everyone is excited. "What does our judge think?" they wonder.

Finally, the judge says, "María Serafina Graciela Mamani, please put three gold coins into my cup."

Oh nooooo! María does not have any gold coins.

But she does have friends! The farmer
puts a gold coin in the cup. The cook puts
one in, too. So does the neighbor.

"Good," the judge says. "Now María can
pay the baker."

Then the judge shakes the cup. "The sound of María's coins pays for the smell of the baker's bread," he says.

The judge gives the coins back to María.
"These are yours," he says. Everyone cheers
and cheers.

Sounds and Smells

The coins make their sounds.
They make their sounds. *Tin, tin!*

The bread leaves its smell.
It leaves its smell. *Mm, mm!*

María keeps her money.
She keeps her money. *Yeee!*

The baker shakes his fist and yells!
He shakes his fist and yells. *Grrr!*

María celebrates with her friends.
They dance and sing. They smell the
bread. Everyone is so happy!